Drums Send a Signal

Chad Taylor

Rosen REAL READERS

Rosen Classroom™
New York

Have you ever used a drum?
Drums make sounds.

A drum is empty inside.
A thin skin covers the top.

When the skin is hit,
it makes a deep sound.

Drums are not all the same.
The size and shape changes
the sound.

Drums are used to keep the beat.

Bands have drums.
The drums help the band
play at the right speed.

Marching bands have drums, too.
They help everyone march together.

Drums Send a Signal

Chad Taylor

Published in 2017 by the Rosen Publishing Group, Inc.
29 East 21st Street, New York, NY 10010

Book Design: Dean Galiano

ISBN: 978-1-5081-2434-4
6-pack ISBN: 978-1-5081-2435-1

Manufactured in the United States of America

Armies once used drums.
They told soldiers how fast
to march.

Some drums are hit with drumsticks.
Some are hit with hands.

It does not matter how they
are played.
Drums send a signal.

Words to Know

army

drum

drumsticks

hands

marching
band

soldier